GOD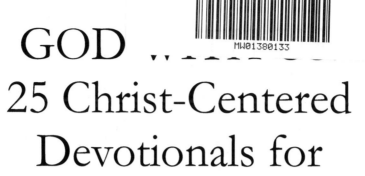
25 Christ-Centered Devotionals for Christmas

RC KUNST

The University of Oxford

RC KUNST

Copyright © 2018 AppliedTruth

All rights reserved.

ISBN: 9781730702457

DEDICATION

This is dedicated to my family for always making Christmas an interesting time of year and always the best time of year. There is no better way to celebrate the birth of the Christ than with a bunch of fun-loving family members.

DISCLAIMER: Self-Publishes books will have errors in spelling, punctuation and so forth. Please be gracious throughout as this book aims not to be perfect but to be an uplifting look at the word of God.

God With Us: 25 Christ-Centered Devotionals for Christmas

CONTENTS

INTRO	iv
Day 1	1
Day 2	3
Day 3	6
Day 4	9
Day 5	12
Day 6	14
Day 7	17
Day 8	20
Day 9	23
Day 10	26
Day 11	28
Day 12	31
Day 13	33
Day 14	35
Day 15	37
Day 16	40
Day 17	43
Day 18	45
Day 19	48
Day 20	51
Day 21	54
Day 22	57
Day 23	59

RC KUNST

Day 24   61

Day 25   64

INTRODUCTION

The entire concept for this devotional came from a small thought I had this last year: "Christmas is pretty routine, I feel like it's just a normal tradition or go through the motions day for everyone." That's not to throw rocks at people or even for one moment consider that I am not partaking in such an attitude because I surely was. However, I want to make a change and in this change I want to focus more on the narrative of Jesus Christ and less on the man centered traditions that consume me during this time of year.

This is a very short and to the point book (or devotional) and it will hopefully be an aid to those seeking to deepen their knowledge on the Christmas story as the Bible tells it and also give you some challenges along the way to apply to your everyday life. I also hope that it's something people can revisit every year to be reminded of the depth and magnitude that the Christmas story beholds. As you step into the 25 days of Christmas or Advent, I hope that you are excited about the events that make this time of year possible.

Enjoy.

RC KUNST

DAY 1
JOHN 1:1

"In the beginning was the Word, and the Word was with God, and the Word was fully God."

In this first day, we encounter the wonderful description of Jesus Christ our Lord. He was in the beginning, without cause; He was the with the Father; He was fully God. The literal reading of the final sentence is: "and what God was the Word was". This is the pinnacle text to the Christmas story, so important, John records it before anything else. All things come from Christ, His words brought everything we know into existence. Therefore, He is the only one fit to redeem us to the Father and reconcile that which was broken long ago in the ancient of days.

Christ pre-existed everything, was without cause and caused all things to be. The Greek renders this precisely: "ἐν ἀρχῇ" as a state of existing, or to say that He simply was and is. The word LOGOS or λόγος is used elsewhere in scripture as "speak, speech or declare" but here it is used for the Christ. This relates us back to the Old Testament where you'll see "the Word of the Lord" used very frequently for divine revelation or God's revealed words.

Now, the "Word of the Lord" or the LOGOS is revealed

through the person of Jesus Christ in His teachings, ministry, death and resurrection. We see John come back to this in verse 14: "And the Word became flesh and dwelt among us, and we saw His glory, glory as of the only begotten from the Father, full of grace and truth." And this is where the start of the Christmas story unfolds. The answer to the questions "who is Jesus?" & "why did He come?"

If we are able to grasp who Jesus is, why He came and so forth we are able to step into the shoes of the disciples who were often asked by our Lord: "Who do you say that I am?" (Matthew 16:15). We see that the Christmas story begins and ends with Jesus, that the story unfolding throughout the narrative of the Old Testament (i.e, the separation caused by sin) sends the Word of the Lord to take on flesh for our sake.

Challenge Questions:

(1) Why is it important to know who Jesus is in relation to the Trinity?

(2) How does this relate to the story of Christmas?

DAY 2
LUKE 1:26-27

"In the sixth month of Elizabeth's pregnancy, the angel Gabriel was sent by God to a town of Galilee called Nazareth, 1:27 to a virgin engaged to a man whose name was Joseph, a descendant of David, and the virgin's name was Mary."

Here we have the beginning of heaven impacting earth through the person and being of Jesus Christ. We have Elizabeth who is pregnant with John the Baptist. The man who would pave the way for the coming ministry of Jesus Christ. So let's jump in to what, on the surface, seems like a verse that doesn't mean much to the Christmas story.

The phrase "in the sixth month" refers to the length of Elizabeth's pregnancy. The verb ἀπεστάλη is important because of the passive. God is the agent of the passive. Two thoughts are evident. From the perspective of the Law, the Annunciation [or the proclaiming of the incarnation] to Mary of the incarnation is nothing less than a proclamation of human godlessness. If man could have saved himself, he wouldn't need a Savior. From the perspective of the Gospel, the sending of Gabriel is a proclamation that God intends to do something to rectify the plight of humanity. Nazareth of Galilee is, humanly speaking, an unlikely place for the announcement of the incarnation to take place. Shouldn't we expect the King of the

3

Jews to come to from royal Jerusalem? The thought of Nathanael is an apt commentary: "Can any good thing come out of Nazareth?" (John 1:46).

The virgin conception and birth is, here, about to be announced (v. 31). The age-old controversy regarding the almah of Isaiah 7:14 is, here, resolved. As if to emphasize this fact, Luke uses "virgin" (παρθένον) twice in this passage. The clear statement of Scripture is that Isaiah's almah is to be understood as a virgin. Decisive in this matter is Matthew 1:23: "Behold, the virgin [παρθένον] shall be with child, and shall bear a Son, and they shall call His name Immanuel" which translated means, "God with us."

"God with us" is the start of our Christmas story, the very beginning of Christ entering into humanity to save the lives of humanity. "God with us" are the first words that kick off the Gospel message that would change the course of history forever. Christ is about to fulfill many prophecies from the Old Testament. First and foremost, the Davidic ancestry found in 2 Sam. 7:12-16, Psalm 89:36, Isaiah 11:1ff., Jer. 23:5-6, Jer. 33:15-17, Matt. 1:1, and Luke 3:31. The author makes it known that both Mary and Jospeh are from the line of David.

Two key aspects to focus on from these passages is that Jesus was born of a virgin which kept him from the Original Sin passing through the blood of Adam. Secondly, the Davidic line was fulfilled, setting up the coming of the Messiah by fulfilling a foretold prophecy even before the child was born. Also note, the Old Testament identified the coming redeemer as Immanuel (meaning "God with us"), Mighty God, Everlasting Father, etc. (Isaiah 9:6; 1:14f); and this identification was continued in the New Testament where Jesus Christ is referred to no less than ten times as "God." How could God have become a man if not by means of a virgin birth? The pre-existence of Christ "before the world was" (John 17:5) made it an impossibility for him to have entered earth life as a result of the normal processes of procreation in which the union of two mortals, male and female, is utterly incapable of producing a life which had already existed. A denial of the virgin birth is a denial of the deity of Jesus Christ.

Challenge Questions:

(1) This Christmas, how can you focus on the name "Immanuel" or "God with us?" Suggestion: Make your Christmas morning centered on reading God's word!

(2) Have you ever pondered how Jesus left divinity to enter humanity? How does that make you appreciate His coming and birth?

DAY 3
LUKE 1:5-6

"During the reign of Herod king of Judea, there lived a priest named Zechariah who belonged to the priestly division of Abijah, and he had a wife named Elizabeth, who was a descendant of Aaron. 1:6 They were both righteous in the sight of God, following all the commandments and ordinances of the Lord blamelessly. 1:7 But they did not have a child, because Elizabeth was barren, and they were both very old."

Here you have the beginning of John the Baptist, who was the way-maker for the Lord Jesus and His ministry. His parents, coming from the line of Aaron, two famous and blameless parents, has shown in his conception to the end that men should be more readily prepared for the hearing of his preaching, according to the forewarning of the prophets. They were commended by God for their moral and sacramental obedience to His statutes.

Now, this is Luke's first and foremost record in his book. The topic is the forerunner of Jesus Christ, as previously mentioned. Before diving into the significance of this for our Christmas moment, there is something else that is Christmas-like in these passages that often goes unknown. The angels of the Lord are so frequent before the ministry of Jesus Christ that it should portray a very distinct picture for us. That Jesus is no angel, but the Lord of angels. These angels who appear to various stewards of God have one thing to say "THE LORD IS

COMING". They come and foretell the coming of their King, Jesus.

John the Baptist, the first prophet called by God in over 400 years. The prophet who would lead the way for the coming Christ on Christmas day. He would take up the mantle of forerunner and fulfill the prophecy found in Isaiah 40:3-5: *"A voice of one calling: 'In the desert prepare the way for the LORD; make straight in the wilderness a highway for our God. Every valley shall be raised up, every mountain and hill made low; the rough ground shall become level, the rugged places a plain. And the glory of the LORD will be revealed, and all mankind together will see it. For the mouth of the LORD has spoken"*. This passage illustrates God's master plan in action as God selected John to be His special ambassador to proclaim His own coming.

John wasn't just foretold and birthed from miraculous parents who were in their elder years. John was related to Jesus Christ himself through their mothers. We won't get into much of what John did within his ministry other than the fact that John lived a rugged, simple life with a focus on the Kingdom coming. John's focus was to fulfill his mission as a forerunner and do so until the day that he died under Herod.

The question now arises, are you a forerunner for Christ second coming? We've been entrusted with the same task as John the Baptist Matthew 28:18–20; John 13:34–35; 1 Peter 3:15; 2 Corinthians 5:16–21. We can follow John's example of faithful and obedient trust in God as we live and proclaim His truth in whatever life circumstances God has given us.

Challenge Questions:

(1) Are you making disciples? Do you have a small ministry in your own life?

(2) This Christmas, with the holiday cheer spreading, can you find a moment to pave the way for Christ by sharing the Gospel with someone?

DAY 4
LUKE 1:39-45

"In those days Mary got up and went hurriedly into the hill country, to a town of Judah, 1:40 and entered Zechariah's house and greeted Elizabeth. 1:41 When Elizabeth heard Mary's greeting, the baby leaped in her womb, and Elizabeth was filled with the Holy Spirit. 1:42 She exclaimed with a loud voice, "Blessed are you among women, and blessed is the child in your womb! 1:43 And who am I that the mother of my Lord should come and visit me? 1:44 For the instant the sound of your greeting reached my ears, the baby in my womb leaped for joy. 1:45 And blessed is she who believed that what was spoken to her by the Lord would be fulfilled."

Here we meet two women (well, actually three) who, moved by the Spirit, raise their voices in praise of God. First is Elizabeth, cousin of Mary, wife of Zechariah (a temple priest in Jerusalem), and mother of John the Baptist. Elizabeth was, like her foremothers Sarah (from the Genesis heritage) and Hannah (from 1 Samuel), unable to have children; until the unexpected birth of John. Elizabeth is not just important because of her family relationships, however. When she greets her pregnant cousin Mary she is filled with the Holy Spirit, and "exclaimed with a loud cry ... " This phrase in Greek means to shout as though one is using a *large horn,* literally a "big" or "mega" voice. This is how Elizabeth speaks a prophetic word to Mary, and so to us -- in her outdoor voice.

Second is Mary (we actually meet her first, but her speech comes second): cousin of Elizabeth, wife of Joseph, mother of Jesus. Like Elizabeth, Mary is important for what she has to say, and not just because of whose mother she is. Mary's song of praise is familiar enough that we need to go in depth here. What is striking, however, is how similar Mary's spiritual situation and words are to those of her cousin Elizabeth.

Mary's rejoicing reflects that of Hannah in 1 Samuel Chapter 2. The exalting of the Lord and His faithfulness to come through for them.

Both Hannah and Mary exclaim their joy in their God. Both Hannah and Mary take heart in the promise (here sung as a declaration of that promise) that the Lord considers, cares for, and acts on behalf of the lowly -- despite what one might expect (and contrary to how we human beings behave ourselves) it is not for kings or the mighty and powerful that the Lord has regard, rather it is for all the rest that God does great things.

Both Hannah and Mary identify what God is doing as being not just for them, but also through them for the whole people.

Both Hannah and Mary sing a song that can be, should be, our song in this Advent season. As we have prepared for the coming of the Christ Child, now we too can sing in thanksgiving, in celebration, in remembrance, and in proclamation of the promise made to our ancestors. Like Hannah, and Mary, and Elizabeth too, this is the time for us to indulge in unadulterated, celebratory joy in the promises that come to us in Jesus. Let us raise our voices in a great cry, magnifying our God.

The leap of John when met with Jesus in the womb is a sudden sign like that found in Genesis 25 where we see the future beckoning of these two wave-makers. One, John that is, as we learned, would be the way maker for Jesus, the second child here. These two children are not only miracles to their respected mothers but miracles to the entire human race. They will change history for the better and die doing so. The Holy Spirit was with them even prior to their birth. We know this especially of Jesus, as He was concealed with the Spirit. However, it's noteworthy to see that John is also filled with the Spirit prior to his birth.

Challenge Questions:

(1) This Christmas, how are you rejoicing in the Lord alongside these women?

(2) Remember this Christmas, the full narrative of Christmas unfolding in the Old Testament and New Testament, will you pray for God to be shown this year?

DAY 5
JEREMIAH 33:14-15

33:14 "I, the Lord, affirm: The time will certainly come when I will fulfill my gracious promise concerning the nations of Israel and Judah. 33:15 In those days and at that time I will raise up for them a righteous descendant of David."

Let us shine some light on the context of today's scripture. This verse, while clearly showing the Light of Christ to come, is coming at at time of great need for Israel. The armies of Nebuchadnezzar, king of Babylon, are advancing on Jerusalem. The streets of Jerusalem will soon be filled with the corpses of her people (33:4-5), and the prophet Jeremiah himself is imprisoned by King Zedekiah (33:1)

And now, in this passage, Jeremiah speaks of the restoration not simply of daily life, but also of one of the chief signs of God's favor, the restoration of the Davidic line. A "righteous branch" will sprout from the line of David. A similar image is found in Isaiah 11:1--"A shoot shall come out from the stump of Jesse, and a branch shall grow out of his roots." The image is one of hope and unexpected joy: new life springing up from what looks like a dead stump.

One of the main strategies of the Babylonian Exile, of course, was the end of the Davidic dynasty. For nearly four hundred years, descendants of David had occupied the throne of Judah, and God had promised that it would always be so (2 Samuel 7; Psalm 89). But the Babylonians destroyed David's city, burned Solomon's temple, and took David's heirs into exile. The promises of God seemed to have come to an end.

A righteous branch will spring up. This is the word of promise that Jeremiah is proclaiming. That the Lord will keep His promise and never abandon a single one. This promise blossomed from a branch into a world-wide tree of life. It is by this very promise that Christ entered the world to save people like you and me. He is the fulfillment in this Advent hope. The same proclamation is given today to us, inheritors of Jeremiah's task. We are called to speak a word of hope and promise in a world often filled with fear and uncertainty, even despair. Especially in this season of Advent, we speak words of hope. In the midst of darkness, light is about to break in. In the midst of despair, hope erupts. After long waiting, a branch will sprout. The complete fulfillment of God's promises has not yet happened, but it is coming. Such is Advent faith, and Advent hope.

Challenge Questions:

(1) How have you seen God be faithful in your everyday life?

(2) This Christmas, is there someone you'd like to share this promise with?

DAY 6
MICAH 5:2

5:2 As for you, Bethlehem Ephrathah,
seemingly insignificant among the clans of Judah—
from you a king will emerge who will rule over Israel on my behalf,
one whose origins are from eternity.

God works some of his most incredible miracles through those who are seen as lowly. Bethlehem was located outside of Jerusalem. It was a small town met with many shepherds. It should be noted, shepherds were often excluded from entering the main city because they were dirty and not seen as normal class citizens.

We know this story well. Jacob, Joseph, David himself-- these are the younger brothers, the ones not supposed to be chosen. In fact, biblical law commands that the older brother gets the birthright, no matter the feelings of the father (Deuteronomy 21:15-17).

And yet, it happens again and again. The youngest is chosen. Jacob gets the birthright and the blessing. Joseph is exalted over his brothers. David is overlooked until all of his brothers have been paraded before Samuel. Then, finally, he is called in from the pastures surrounding Bethlehem to stand before the prophet and be anointed king (1 Samuel 16).

God does it again. God chooses the unlikely place and the unlikely people to work through. He refuses to give up on the lowly in order to make His great name known. It is a consistent theme through the Bible that God delights in upsetting human expectations. Abraham and Sarah did not expect to bear a child in old age, and yet Isaac, whose name means "he laughs," was such a preposterous surprise that it prompted Sarah's laughter (Genesis 20:1-7). David, who was the smallest of his brothers, was anointed as the king (1 Samuel 16). The ruler promised in Micah's oracle comes from an unexpected place in an unexpected way. This divine habit of eschewing expectations also echoes in the New Testament, as Mary receives a surprise announcement that she will bear a child (Luke 1) and as Jesus enters the world not as a triumphant ruler but as a vulnerable child.

The irony of Advent is that this season of preparation anticipates a hopeful expectation of that which is unexpected. Those who have heard these Scriptures so many times, year after year of Advent celebration, may have trouble fully appreciating their startling logic. Yet perhaps we need look no further than our own lives. Micah calls us to see God's faithfulness in surprising ways, to look where we might not expect. Micah's oracle serves as a reminder that the promise of God's covenant is certain, yet the expression of its fulfillment is not always predictable.

As Proverbs says "man plans his steps but the LORD directs his ways". We can plan out everything, even centered on the Word of God, which is how we should live our lives, but we never truly know the way we will get there. God uses underdogs, God uses the lowly, God seeks the humble and the meek.

Remember two things this Christmas, if nothing else. Remember that when you feel worthless in the eyes of the world, you are worth more than life itself in the eyes of Jesus. Second, remember those who don't have what you have this Christmas, remember that what we do for them we do for the Lord.

Challenge Questions:

(1) How can you serve someone this Christmas who has less?

(2) When is the last time you felt less than worthy? did you go to Christ or something else? Challenge: Go to Christ first. Not as a last resort.

DAY 7
ISAIAH 11:1-2

¹ Out of the stump of David's family will grow a shoot—
yes, a new Branch bearing fruit from the old root.
² And the Spirit of the Lord will rest on him—
the Spirit of wisdom and understanding,
the Spirit of counsel and might,
the Spirit of knowledge and the fear of the Lord.

We saw a couple of days ago that Jeremiah spoke of a branch shooting out that would become Righteous. This prophecy proclaims the coming of someone who will heir from the Davidic line and will rest upon the Lord.

On a more historical note, we can find it interesting how this text goes against the normal king's propaganda found in that time. In the royal propaganda of the ancient near East, royal figures frequently encounter predatory animals, and especially lions. And so it is no surprise to find the royal child depicted as a shepherd among lions. What is surprising, however, is the way in which the young shepherd interacts with them. In general, kings would be depicted fighting and killing lions, not leading them or living among them.

The killing of lions demonstrated one's worthiness to rule, and was a sign of divine favor. For example, in his bid to fight Goliath David demonstrates his royal credibility when he says to Saul, "Your servant used to keep sheep for his father; and whenever a lion or a bear came, and took a lamb from the

17

flock, I went after it and struck it down, rescuing the lamb from its mouth; and if it turned against me, I would catch it by the jaw, strike it down, and kill it. Your servant has killed both lions and bears; and this uncircumcised Philistine shall be like one of them, since he has defied the armies of the living God." David said, "The Lord, who saved me from the paw of the lion and from the paw of the bear, will save me from the hand of this Philistine" (1 Sam 17:34-37). The foreshadowing at work here is obvious: David was not only acting like a shepherd; he was acting like a king. Unlike his ancient Near Eastern contemporaries, however, the Davidic ruler of Isaiah 11 does not hunt lions. Rather, he mysteriously remakes them. And he does so in a way that utterly eliminates predatory violence from the food chain. For Isaiah 11, these are the fruits of the just and righteous reign of David's descendants.

In calling the Messiah a Rod from the stem of Jesse, the LORD is emphasizing the humble nature of the Messiah. Jesse was the much less famous father of King David. It is far more humble to say "from Jesse" than to say "from King David." This text goes further describing 7 attributes of the Spirit that will be upon Him. You must find this to be interesting as these seven aspects of the Spirit of God are not the only characteristics of the Holy Spirit. But they are grouped together in a "seven" to show the fullness and perfection of the Holy Spirit. He will be without sin. That is also predicted there.

It's in this incredible passage that we find the deity of Christ come to life. We know that He will enter humanity on a mission to fulfill the justice of the Father through a sinless life. It's so important to note that the Gospel is not just that Christ died for us, but also that He lived a righteous life for us. He lived the life we could not live and died the death we could not die.

It's in this we find the message of Christmas come to a pinnacle point. One that we must dwell on, rejoice in and pray through. Therefore, in conclusion today there will be no Challenge questions but rather those three challenges. Dwell on this scripture and the 7 attributes. Rejoice in the Lord that He came to live a righteous life for you. Pray through this text and others this Advent season.

DAY 8
ISAIAH 42:1-7

42:1 *"Here is my servant whom I support,*
my chosen one in whom I take pleasure. I have placed my spirit on him; he will
make just decrees for the nations. *42:2* *He will not cry out or shout; he will not*
publicize himself in the streets. *42:3* *A crushed reed he will not break, a dim*
wick he will not extinguish; he will faithfully make just decrees. *42:4* *He will not*
grow dim or be crushed before establishing justice on the earth; the coastlands
will wait in anticipation for his decrees." *42:5* *This is what the true God, the*
Lord, says— the one who created the sky and stretched it out, the one who
fashioned the earth and everything that lives on it, the one who gives breath to
the people on it, and life to those who live on it: *42:6* *"I, the Lord, officially*
commission you; I take hold of your hand. I protect you and make you a
covenant mediator for people, and a light to the nations, *42:7* *to open blind eyes,*
to release prisoners from dungeons, those who live in darkness from prisons.

Christ is foretold thousands of years prior to his birth here as the "chosen one". That's a Christmas story unfolding throughout the narrative of the Bible in the Old Testament! How incredible to think about.

In Isaiah 42, the divine announcer tells of the presence of a servant who is chosen by God and a source of delight for God. God will place God's spirit upon this servant so that the servant is able to bring forth justice to the nations, to be a light, to open blind eyes and bring out prisoners and give truth. In Matthew 3, when Jesus is baptized, God's spirit likewise descends upon him and God delights in him. The relationship here is not between God and God's servant, but between God and God's beloved son: "This is my son, the Beloved, with whom I am well pleased"

So when you look at the word servant there we can directly connect that with Jesus. The New King James Version rightly capitalizes **Servant**, because the context demonstrates this is a clear reference to Jesus. Additionally, Matthew quotes Isaiah 42:1-5 and plainly says it is a prophecy fulfilled in Jesus (Matthew 12:16-21). So in this, the LORD commands all peoples to put their focus on Jesus.

We further verify that Christ tells of Himself, to be the Servant: Jesus described Himself as a servant in Matthew 20:25-28, Matthew 23:11, Mark 9:35, Mark 10:43-45. Peter, in his Acts 3 sermon, gives our Savior the title *His Servant Jesus* (Acts 3:13 and 3:26). In Acts 4, the praying people of God speak of *Your holy Servant Jesus* (Acts 4:27, 4:30). But Jesus isn't just *a* servant. He is *The Servant*, and every one should **behold**, as the LORD says, **My Servant**.

This further is enunciated in the text by God calling Him "my chosen one" or more literally: "my ELECT One" to which we can see that election is about being chosen in Christ and to become like Christ, the ultimate servant.

Christmas is a time when people think about serving others more often than not. Not everyone, but a lot of people change their hearts toward the down-rotten this time of year. I know for myself, I always go overboard with gift giving to my nieces, my nephews and the rest of my family. There is something about serving others in various ways during Christmas that makes us feel an immense joy. That doesn't have to be the case once a year. The eggnog doesn't make you a giver, the Giver makes you a giver. He has placed in us a desire to serve. He has placed in us a desire to be LIKE Christ. In fact, He has elected us to become like Christ.

Remember that becoming like Christ isn't always happy or easy. Becoming more like Christ is tough but joyful. It is our ultimate purpose and we should reflect on this during this time of year. Remember Christ as the Ultimate Servant and what He was born to do.

Challenge Questions:

(1) How can we better serve those near us this year?

(2) How did Jesus serve those around Him?

(3) How can we reflect that?

DAY 9
JOHN 1:29

1:29 On the next day John saw Jesus coming toward him and said, "Look, the Lamb of God who takes away the sin of the world!

We've looked at the birth and coming messenger of John the Baptist but here we have need of him in a greater sense. Here John exclaims the profound truth to the hilltops. This is the message of the Christ and Christmas all wrapped up in a short verse. *The Lamb of God* is not just a humble title that Christ carries but it's the truth behind such a title that gives it purpose. Christ is going to the ultimate sacrifice for all of mankind. He is going to die upon the cross just 30 some years after coming into the world that He, Himself, created. This allusion [A figure of speech that makes an implied or indirect reference to literature, culture, history, etc., leaving the reader or hearer to make the connection] to the symbolism of the Passover lamb (Exod 12:3) is something that we often miss reference to. There would be no reconciliation if Jesus had not become the "Lamb come for slaughter."

The sins of the world is a statement that, in that day, was known to mankind but for anyone to come and say they forgive sins would be a "blasphemy". In fact, Jesus is accused of this later in Matthew chapter 9 - where some of the teachers of the Law hear Jesus say: "Take heart, son; your sins are forgiven." Only God could forgive sins and we see that not only does Christ not refuse the ability to forgive sins but He alone owns it. The Lamb who came to die for sin also forgives our sins but one day will relinquish the world of sin. He is the author and perfecter of all these things and all that is to be made holy will be made holy through Him.

There are many miracles that come directly from the Christmas story but there is one that I am trying to lay emphasis on throughout this study. It is that Christ, leaving divinity, enters humanity and dies for our sins. It is the Gospel of Jesus Christ that I want to emphasize. Often in life we go through the motions but this is true of Christmas too. I know that I am guilty of it - I often find myself shopping for others, looking for decorations, getting excited about all the hot chocolate and cookies. I'm looking forward to spending time with family and making new memories. I go through the "Jingle Bell Motions" or in other words, I enjoy too much of a holiday without remembering the purpose of such a holiday.

I'm writing this so many of you may center your focus on Christ and the things of Christ this year but I am also writing to myself here. As Christians we should make Christ the center of our lives every single day but often it takes a holiday like Christmas to center ourselves into Him. Now, I am not saying not to enjoy the things that this holiday brings - please go watch Elf at least five times...I know I will be. All I am trying to get across is that we should make the Gospel message a focus during the holiday too. Maybe we make a new tradition that will catch fire during the Season of Christmas and carry on for generations. Simply put - do a new motion this year and make it centered around Christ.

Challenge Question:

(1) Are you guilty of going through the motions? If so, how can you better change your focus?

DAY 10
MATTHEW 1:18-25

"Now the birth of Jesus Christ happened this way. While his mother Mary was engaged to Joseph, but before they came together, she was found to be pregnant through the Holy Spirit. 1:19 Because Joseph, her husband to be, was a righteous man, and because he did not want to disgrace her, he intended to divorce her privately. 1:20 When he had contemplated this, an angel of the Lord appeared to him in a dream and said, "Joseph, son of David, do not be afraid to take Mary as your wife, because the child conceived in her is from the Holy Spirit. 1:21 She will give birth to a son and you will name him Jesus, because he will save his people from their sins." 1:22 This all happened so that what was spoken by the Lord through the prophet would be fulfilled: 1:23 "Look! The virgin will conceive and bear a son, and they will call him Emmanuel," which means "God with us." 1:24 When Joseph awoke from sleep he did what the angel of the Lord told him. He took his wife, 1:25 but did not have marital relations with her until she gave birth to a son, whom he named Jesus."

This section is, of course, one of the prime passages used and preached on during the Christmas season. The challenge is to say something fresh but yet familiar and reassuring about it.

An important exegetical perspective that needs to be kept in mind is the Matthew text tells the story more from the angle of Joseph's perspective, while the Luke birth narrative tells the tale from the perspective of how things affected and were seen by Mary. The virgin birth and incarnation are two hefty doctrines that are pinnacles to the Christian faith and the Christmas narrative. The raise questions and one of those would be "why did God come to be with man?" this question can be answered in an array of ways but let us focus on one answer, that is, to reveal Himself to a fallen mankind.

The fulfillment of Scripture is also seen here. Yesterday we looked at Isaiah 7:14 and today we see it fulfilled in Matthew v23. This wonderful and strange miracle is starting to unfold through the lives of Mary and Jospeh. This is a narrative of surprising and unexpected events and suggests a God of unexpected actions. God uses His past word to fulfill His present word and that is an important exegetical practice for us today. Allow the Bible to interpret itself.

It should also be noted the stories thereafter (see e.g. Mark 3:21-35 and Mark 6 and the parallels in Matthew) suggest Mary and Joseph, being good early Jews, went on to have numerous children, both boys and girls the natural way who are rightly called Jesus' brothers and sisters. In short, Matthew's Gospel affirms the virginal conception of Mary, but not her perpetual virginity.

Challenge Questions:

(1) God works in strange ways, have you seen Him work through someone in your life lately?

(2) If not, pray that God will work through you in someone else's life. Are you willing?

DAY 11
LUKE 2:1-3

Now in those days a decree went out from Caesar Augustus to register all the empire for taxes. 2:2 This was the first registration, taken when Quirinius was governor of Syria. 2:3 Everyone went to his own town to be registered.

The days of the birth of the long expected Messiah. God is completely sovereign over the events unfolding in History and this is never more apparent than the story of Christmas. Proverbs says that "The king's heart is like channels of water in the hand of the LORD; He turns it wherever He wishes" (Proverbs 21:1) and so in Luke's account we see God moving the heart of Augustus who, by his edict calling for a census, sets the historical stage for the Messiah to be born in Bethlehem. God through the sovereign action caused Joseph to go from Nazareth to Bethlehem in order to fulfill Micah 5:2 which we've previously seen.

We must always remind ourselves that the Bible records *actual history* and *real events*. This is not "once upon a time." This is not fanciful stories of Zeus and Apollo on Mount Olympus. This is *real*. The stories unfolding are God's deliberate plan for redemption that includes the plans He has for us today. He is the ultimate guide, the ultimate purpose and reason for this season.

The world of Caesar Augustus was one that was prepping for the need of a Savior like Jesus Christ. It was wrought with war, killing, sexual immorality and more. That also lead to the Pax Romana which allowed for religious and ideas to spread across the seas. The "registration" and census described wasn't for simple record-keeping or statistics. It was to efficiently and effectively tax everyone in the Roman Empire. Now for an absolutely incredible fact that we should all hold as significant: Justin Martyr, writing in the middle of the second century, said that in his own day, more than a hundred years after the time of Jesus, you could look up the registers of the same census Luke mentions.

The journey was about to be a hard one for Joseph and Mary as they leave their home behind to return to follow the order of the census. This was all part of God's divine plan. There is something interesting here that I am thinking about as I write this. The fact that in grade school I studied the Caesar's and their history. The interesting thing about secular history is that it only tells part of the story. The census and the move of Joseph and Mary is as much history as anything else we've studied.

Challenge Questions:

(1) Do you believe that History is governed not by just man but by the Sovereign God?

(2) Imagine traveling like Joseph and Mary had to - what are some things that would enter your mind?

DAY 12
LUKE 2:4-7

2:4 So Joseph also went up from the town of Nazareth in Galilee to Judea, to the city of David called Bethlehem, because he was of the house and family line of David. 2:5 He went to be registered with Mary, who was promised in marriage to him, and who was expecting a child. 2:6 While they were there, the time came for her to deliver her child. 2:7 And she gave birth to her firstborn son and wrapped him in strips of cloth and laid him in a manger, because there was no place for them in the inn.

Calmly, Luke tells the story of the birth of Jesus. In our hearts and our eyes, we see the Son of God and the redemptive Christ being born in strips of cloth and lying in a manger. This is actually something I grew rather numb to because it didn't seem like a huge deal after growing up in a Christian home where every Christmas it was sung or talked about "baby boy jesus....la la la". However, taking this into account post-theology degree - I find it to be much more interesting.

Jesus Christ, our King and Savior, started not in a Kingdom here on earth but in a manger. Christ didn't leave one Kingdom and enter into another. He entered into humanity in full humility, in full humanity and in a way that would define who He is to others in His coming ministry. This is a picture of the Savior that we should not neglect but embrace and look at deeply. Jesus' birth took place in humble conditions, foreshadowing that Jesus will not be given a king's proper welcome. The endearing setting of a Christmas manger scene may cause us to forget that Jesus is the glorious King of kings. We routinely offer God less than He truly deserves. Let us confess our deficient response to our majestic Lord and commit to conduct worthy of God's incarnate Son.

Entirely alone, Mary, brings forth the promised son that she so long awaited. The famous song "Mary, Did you know?" comes to my mind when I read over this. She must of known that Jesus was about to be different, about to change the course of History and be like no other man ever before or ever to be. Right?

This day is simple - do not let the grander and the miraculous event of Jesus' birth go under appreciated. Gather your heart and set before you time to pray. There is no Challenge questions for this just a call to reflect on the majesty and humility combined together that brought Jesus into the world so that He may reconcile us to the Father. And how it all started on a Christmas night.

DAY 13
LUKE 2:8-14

2:8 Now there were shepherds nearby living out in the field, keeping guard over their flock at night. 2:9 An angel of the Lord appeared to them, and the glory of the Lord shone around them, and they were absolutely terrified. 2:10 But the angel said to them, "Do not be afraid! Listen carefully, for I proclaim to you good news that brings great joy to all the people: 2:11 Today your Savior is born in the city of David. He is Christ the Lord. 2:12 This will be a sign for you: You will find a baby wrapped in strips of cloth and lying in a manger." 2:13 Suddenly a vast, heavenly army appeared with the angel, praising God and saying, 2:14 "Glory to God in the highest, and on earth peace among people with whom he is pleased!"

Imagine minding your own business at work and all of a sudden a mystical angel appears and demands to tell you good news. This is a scene not out of Bruce Almighty but right out of Scripture that shows us a grand scene but there is something else here that is happening. Something the normal reader will most likely miss or overlook. Something that could change our perspective forever.

Shepherds were despised by the orthodox good people of the day. They were quite unable to keep the details of the ceremonial law; they could not observe all the meticulous hand-washings and rules and regulations. Their flocks made far too constant demands on them; and so the orthodox looked down on them. It was to simple men of the fields that God's message first came. God did two unthinkable things in one night (if not more…) He was born into humanity in a lowly manger and He sent an angel to speak to one of the most neglected groups of men. This should give us pause and praise. Pause because it is an unworthy gesture of the Lord to save people like us - wretched sinners are we. Praise because He did not overlook what we overlook, He sees all in need and all have a chance to be redeemed to the Father through the Lord Jesus Christ because of what took place on Christmas.

Just like the angel changed the lowly shepherds lives that night by giving them a hope and a reason - Jesus too gives us a hope and reason. The other interesting thing about the location of these shepherds was that they were in distance of Bethlehem which means they were most likely the shepherds who were responsible for providing the lamb of slaughter for the Temple sacrifices. Fitting that they'd be chosen to go see the Lamb who would be killed for the atonement of all mankind.

Challenge Questions:

(1) Do you think yourself to be less than? If so, remember today that God views you as important and worth it.

(2) Think of someone who has less than you - maybe someone in school, work or wherever that is cast out by the general groups. How can you reflect Christ love to them this Christmas?

DAY 14
LUKE 2:15-16

2:15 When the angels left them and went back to heaven, the shepherds said to one another, "Let us go over to Bethlehem and see this thing that has taken place, that the Lord has made known to us." 2:16 So they hurried off and located Mary and Joseph, and found the baby lying in a manger.

As you may have expected, after seeing an angel commanding you to go see the Savior of the world - you scurry off in urgency. These men didn't waste a moment. They left on that Christmas night to find the King that would set them free, the Lamb that would end all sacrifices and the God whom they serve.

The specific sign was not the common "baby wrapped in swaddling cloth" but rather that the baby was in a manger. This was the uncommon thread found in the reliability testimony of the angel. The shepherds then knew what to look for and when they'd find it. What a strange sight for all who came across this - the King of the Jews, the Savior of the World, the God of the Universe lie crying in the manger having entered the world through the most lowly of ways.

Visited by shepherds is even more fitting, not just to conceal the lowly entry of God into humanity, but that Christ would both be the lamb for slaughter and the shepherd of many. He would herd many to Himself throughout His ministry but even more through the coming ages. The story of Christmas rings through the timeline of history without fading a single note.

On a more applicable level, I find myself rarely eager some days to study what Christ said, did and will do (or the Bible). I find myself much like everyone else in Bethlehem on Christmas Day - within the realm of Christ but not fixated on what is actually going on. However, the days that I am eager and zealous to seek Christ in the manger (rather, study His words) I can feel the grace overcoming. I pray that we fuel that fire in all of our hearts this coming year.

To be more eager to run to the manger in awe. To be more excited to hear the words of the King. To cherish the moments that we have to read the Word of God and see it fulfilled in history, our lives and coming days. I pray this to the Lord for all of humanity.

Challenge Questions:

(1) How often are you excited for Christ and His return? Is it something you think about regularly?

(2) Pray over your study time and quietly ask the Lord to fuel your heart for Him.

DAY 15
LUKE 2:17-20

After seeing him, the shepherds told everyone what had happened and what the angel had said to them about this child. 18 All who heard the shepherds' story were astonished, 19 but Mary kept all these things in her heart and thought about them often. 20 The shepherds went back to their flocks, glorifying and praising God for all they had heard and seen. It was just as the angel had told them.

The shepherds told everyone. The shepherds told everyone. The shepherds told everyone. I repeat this three times because it is something that I never want to forget and I want us to remember as a church. They did not just sit on the miracle or what the angels revealed to them. Oh, how often we just sit quietly with our friends without telling them of the glorious and wondrous Gospel of Jesus Christ.

Too often we ponder the questions of acceptance, denial, comparison and so forth. These things only hinder us from fulfilling our eternal destiny of sharing the Good News. As Paul said, "I am not here to please man." We must insist with our minds that the Gospel is worth sharing. The coming of God into humanity out of pure and perfect love. If you could think for a moment - this Christmas - not everyone has love. There are so many people left alone. If you see someone or know someone like this - wouldn't you rationalize that they'd like to hear they are loved?

Simply put, there is no better way to share true love with

someone than to share the Gospel of Jesus Christ with them. Nothing warms the heart like it. We are called to do this, primed and furnished to do the work of the Lord which is sharing His testimony to the masses. But all of this starts with sharing it with one person. Not everyone is Billy Graham, who reaches millions of people, but some of us need to step out in discomfort and share the truth in love with our friends, our family, our coworkers and anyone who needs to hear it.

We have a contrast in the following phrase. We see that Mary kept all these things in her heart to cherish. She meditated on all that had happened to her. All that would happen and all that God promised to her. She was seeing the Hand of God unfold in front of her. This is the second part of what we are called to do. We are called to cherish the word of God and the message He brings. Called to rest and meditate upon it. This story contributes both sides of our calling. One is to share the message to all and the other is to mediate on God's word day in and day out. In doing this, we honor and fulfill the Christmas story, the coming of the Christ.

Challenge Questions:

(1) When is the last time you shared the Gospel? Today we have social media. In the back of this book you'll find a simple paragraph that shares the Gospel truth, will you share it?

(2) When is the last time you meditated on God's word? Take time today to just think on His word. Read a Psalm. Pray through it.

DAY 16
MATTHEW 2:1-2

After Jesus was born in Bethlehem in Judea, in the time of King Herod, wise men from the East came to Jerusalem 2:2 saying, "Where is the one who is born king of the Jews? For we saw his star when it rose and have come to worship him."

Matthew starts off by telling us that Jesus, in the time of Herod, was born in Bethlehem which provides for us a fulfillment of prophecy and a little insight of how Jesus intended to serve while on earth. In one word - humble. Bethlehem was ancestral home of David, the great king of Israel and founder of their royal dynasty. However, it was not a large or significant town. Bethlehem was quite a little town six miles to the south of Jerusalem. Which means Jesus didn't come storming in through the ages, into a kingdom, into a throne or anything like that. He's not a rockstar being born in the L.A.

Jesus has yet to speak a word and he's already radiating the eternal nature that He alone beholds. These shepherd and wise men have come from afar to see the coming of the King in His very first moments. The precious child who would one day sacrifice Himself for everyone born of Adam.

This scene unfolding is the epitome of Christmas. We all are thinking "precious born Jesus" who is surrounded with essential oils and being worshipped. It's quite the sight to imagine, it's something that washes over Christmas without much thought. These astronomers who are at the feet of Jesus, baby feet at

40

that, were not just three wise men, but a great company of them and came later in the months to come.

Sometimes we over traditionalize things and we miss the essential things that the Bible records. Being *from the East*, they would have been among Jews who were exiled from Judah and Israel centuries before. That many Jews were mixed with this people there is little doubt; and that these eastern *magi*, or philosophers, astrologers, or whatever else they were, might have been *originally* of that class, there is room to believe. These, knowing the promise of the Messiah, were now, probably, like other believing Jews, waiting for the consolation of Israel.

However, tradition even tell us their names - supposedly Melchior, Caspar, and Balthasar. You can see their supposed skulls in the great cathedral at Cologne, Germany. These men lead a company to see the baby Jesus who at this time was a few months old. These days, if someone asks me to come see their baby and its a few miles away - I'm making an excuse like "sorry, I...have a dog and...she needs to go outside." Something lame, but showcasing the obvious fact that I don't want to be there. But this baby, brought many visitors, many believers and many from far far away. In fact, a deeper look into this verse we see something spectacular.

For we have seen His star in the East: There are many different suggestions for the natural origin of this remarkable star. Some say it was a conjunction of Jupiter and Saturn, some other planetary conjunctions; others suggest a supernova, and some think of comets or a specifically created unique star or sign. Either way you look at it, Christ was using what He created ages before to relate to these astronomers and speak to them. God relates to who we are, who He has called us to be and will get us to where we need to be BY HIS OWN MEANS, not our own. He fulfills Numbers 24:17 here and in dramatic fashion.

Let that sink in: God will meet you where you are and guide you where you need to go by His own created means.

No questions today, just reflect on that and pray that God will guide you with His guiding light.

DAY 17
MATTHEW 2:3-8

2:3 When King Herod heard this he was alarmed, and all Jerusalem with him. 2:4 After assembling all the chief priests and experts in the law, he asked them where the Christ was to be born. 2:5 "In Bethlehem of Judea," they said, "for it is written this way by the prophet: 2:6 'And you, Bethlehem, in the land of Judah, are in no way least among the rulers of Judah, for out of you will come a ruler who will shepherd my people Israel.' " 2:7 Then Herod privately summoned the wise men and determined from them when the star had appeared. 2:8 He sent them to Bethlehem and said, "Go and look carefully for the child. When you find him, inform me so that I can go and worship him as well."

Here we see Herod introduced in a more dramatic way. Herod was constantly on guard against threats to his rule, especially from his own family. He assassinated many family members whom he suspected of disloyalty. The fact that all Jerusalem was troubled with Herod is significant. This was due either to the fact that the people of Jerusalem rightly feared what sort of paranoid outburst might come from Herod upon hearing of a rival king being born, or because of the size and dignity of this caravan from the East.

This was the first contact the religious leaders had with Jesus. They understood the Biblical information correctly, but failed in Challenge to their lives, which is a significant sign of what is to come. People hear the message, know the theology but ultimately deny the savior by not applying the good news to their lives. The scribes here weren't just recorders of the Old

Testament, they are the ones who taught it every single day.

It should be noted that they knew where he would be born because of Micah 5:2, which they quote to Herod. It's alarming that they knew this but seemingly had no interest at all in finding Jesus. They had correct information, they knew what to say but they denied the urgency to find the Savior. You can be extremely smart, wise and know theology but if you deny the savior, it rings hollow. This is something I repeatedly need to pound into my own mind as someone who teaches theology, holds degrees in theology and loves theology. I must first and foremost be a man of the Gospel and not be quick to "theologize" everything.

As we expect, Herod tries to demise a plan to kill the boy Jesus. He portrays a man wanting to worship Jesus but really wants to end any possibility of Jesus reigning over him. How true of many of us prior to our salvation. Not so much that we wish to kill Jesus but we may want to deny Him any authority over our lives because we live in a culture that demands we do things our own way. As we saw yesterday, we must allow God to guide us by His own terms and means. Submitting to Jesus as LORD and KING is a major part of the Christian's walk.

Challenge Question:
(1) Have you submitted to God's authority over your life? Pray this today. That God may have authority of every aspect of your life.

DAY 18
MATTHEW 2:9-12

2:9 After listening to the king they left, and once again the star they saw when it rose led them until it stopped above the place where the child was. 2:10 When they saw the star they shouted joyfully. 2:11 As they came into the house and saw the child with Mary his mother, they bowed down and worshiped him. They opened their treasure boxes and gave him gifts of gold, frankincense, and myrrh. 2:12 After being warned in a dream not to return to Herod, they went back by another route to their own country.

Here again we see that Christ's creation is in His command. The start or planetary object stops above where Christ is resting. The wise men and company rejoiced when the start had stopped. Their journey was about to conclude at the feet of their Savior. They were about to walk into a miracle, the virgin woman who gave birth to the Son of God. What is the first act that we see the men do? They bow before the King and worship Him, even though Jesus is barely a year old, if that.

The idea that there were three wise men comes from the fact that there were three gifts. We may say that gold speaks of royalty, incense speaks of divinity, and myrrh speaks of death. Yet it is almost certain that the Magi did this unawares; they simply wanted to honor the King of the Jews. The precious gifts were not presented to Mary or Joseph, but to Jesus Himself. Yet undeniably, the infant Jesus did not use or spend any of these precious gifts, but His parents used them, hopefully wisely, on His behalf and benefit. In the same way when we give to Jesus today we do not give to Him directly, but to His people, who use those gifts on His behalf and benefit.

This Christmas you'll be giving gifts of love, thought and kindness. You'll most likely go overboard, if you can. I know that every year I tell myself that I won't spend as much as last year on my nieces, nephews and family but it always fails. I enjoy giving them gifts, I enjoy seeing them happy, I enjoy thinking of things that other people may not think of buying for themselves. Every year it's a small project to think of what to get my father and my brother in law - everyone else is easy.

However, I always need to check myself when I am getting gifts for my loved ones. I have to remember God's loved ones who have less this year. We as a church are called to take care of this who have less and who are in need. Not just once a year but year round. Christ says later in His ministry, " whatever you do for the least of these, you do for me." It's this mentality that we must obtain this Christmas.

If we look at the two accounts of this story between Luke and Matthew we find something outstanding. Jesus comes to the poor (shepherds) first and then the learned and rich (the wise men). As Spurgeon says, ""Those who look for Jesus will see him: those who truly see him will worship him: those who worship him will consecrate their substance to him." and this is a simply but profound truth we must rest on.

46

Challenge Question:

(1) Who can you seek out this Christmas and give a gift of thoughtfulness? Try and think of someone who isn't on your normal radar.

DAY 19
LUKE 1:46-50

1:46 And Mary said, "My soul exalts the Lord, 1:47 and my spirit has begun to rejoice in God my Savior, 1:48 because he has looked upon the humble state of his servant. For from now on all generations will call me blessed, 1:49 because he who is mighty has done great things for me, and holy is his name; 1:50 from generation to generation he is merciful to those who fear him.

Today we get to the counter part of the Hymn of Hannah found in the Old Testament. Mary is proclaiming a prayer in song that exalts Her coming Lord in all of His glory. She does not see herself to be one of worthiness but rather one who is a servant and vessel for the project of God. The verb μεγαλυνειν (magnify or exalt) signifies to celebrate with words, to extol with praises. This is the only way in which God can be magnified, or made great; for, strictly speaking, nothing can be added to God, for he is infinite and eternal; therefore the way to magnify him is to come forth and celebrate those acts in which he has manifested his greatness.

Again, we don't see Mary speaking on her own worthiness but rather that she too, a sinner, is found to be saved in the coming Christ. He is her savior as well as ours. This is a wonderful portrayal and reminder that we are all vessels of God to be used for His glory. Just remember that where you are in life is not a mistake but can be used for God's eternal glory and purpose. I know that I often struggle with this - this idea that I could always be doing more and greater and comparing myself to these big name authors or pastors. But God has me here, in Michigan, in Starbucks, writing my concerns and thoughts about Christmas to whoever ends up reading this devotional, all because He died for me.

Mary further compounds that she not be worshipped or seen as special but rather that she is happy to be a servant. Abraham was blessed in being the father of the faithful; Paul in being the apostle to the Gentiles; Peter in first preaching the gospel to them; but who would think of worshipping or praying to Abraham, Paul, or Peter? I say this not to cut people off whom are raised in the Roman church but rather remind them of Mary's own words before Christmas occurred. She was a servant and a blessed servant at that. May we follow in her wise footsteps. She refers to the Mighty One who is responsible for saving her, using her and blessing her.

She finishes this prayer with a powerful reminder: God blesses those and is merciful to those who fear Him (fear in the sense of reverence, understanding His words and following them). This is a wonderful time of year that we must not forget the main purpose of this year is the coming savior for mankind. Let us remember this in reverence by sharing the Gospel fervently.

Challenge Questions:

(1) Who can you share the Good News with?

(2) What are some fears you have with sharing the Good News?

(3) How can you conquer such fears?

DAY 20
LUKE 1:67-72

1:67 Then his father Zechariah was filled with the Holy Spirit and prophesied, 1:68 "Blessed be the Lord God of Israel, because he has come to help and has redeemed his people. 1:69 For he has raised up a horn of salvation for us in the house of his servant David, 1:70 as he spoke through the mouth of his holy prophets from long ago, 1:71 that we should be saved from our enemies, and from the hand of all who hate us. 1:72 He has done this to show mercy to our ancestors, and to remember his holy covenant.

There is an ironic Christmas clash here. If you recall the movie 'Miracle on 34th street' you'll remember a mental pinning between the skeptic and the miracle believer. That's sort of what happens here in the life of Zechariah.

This song's theology holds a perfect tone for our Christmas season. The song rehearses fidelity of "the Lord God of Israel" to the divine promises spoken in the Old Testament and fulfilled in Jesus. What more perfect message can there be for Advent? We get to see the joyous unfolding of Christ coming to the world. Literally, Joy to the World. Socrates taught for 40 years, but his life and teaching have made no songs. Plato taught for 50 years, but he did nothing to cause the human soul to blossom with life. Yet, Jesus came and lived for only 33 years on this earth and taught only three years. His teachings, as well as His Person, His Promises, and His Power have inspired the souls of Raphael, Michelangelo and Leonardo de Vinci to paint glorious scenes; the hearts of Dante and Milton and Donne to erupt in poetic verse; and the Songs-O the greatest music and

Songs of the Ages came from those whose lives were touched by Christ: Haydn, Handel, Bach, and Mendelssohn. All of these men composed to the praise of Jesus Christ. Indeed, it is said that Jesus Christ changed Mendelssohn's music from a minor key to a major key.

Zechariah was the father of John the Baptist. Like so many key figures in the Old Testament drama, Zechariah was an aged priest. And like so many of those Old Testament figures, Zechariah was childless. He and his wife Elizabeth were childless. We are told that Elizabeth was a "relative" of Mary, meaning that she was part of the same kinship group as Mary. On top of all these notes on Zechariah, the man was mute. He was mute because of his disloyalty and skeptic attitude to an ANGEL APPEARING TO HIM. Why is that emphasized? That's because I want to make this very clear theological point here: Man has the ability and the idiocy to deny God even when man is given a sure sign from God. Therefore, Gabriel pressed the mute button on Zechariah, literally.

This song was not just any old song but rather a Spirit-Filled lyric masterpiece that was meant for prophesying. The phrase translated "spoke this prophecy" is an inelegant and inexact rendering of the Greek (*epropheiteusen legon*), which more precisely means "he prophesied, saying ..." The point being that the speech is not a prophecy, as if "a prophecy" were a thing or prediction, but rather that the speech itself was spirit-event, a moment of God's Holy Spirit breaking into the ordinary, mundane world. And bringing with it God's preferred and promised future.

Christ is near and John the Baptist would pave the way for him. He would be the messenger with a divine purpose coming to set the way for the One who would reconcile all to Himself. And when the first Christmas morn was dawning, the tender mercy of our God broke into the darkness of this world for all. That light still shines in the darkness. And the darkness cannot overcome it.

Challenge Questions:

(1) If God sent a messenger in angelic form for you - would you listen? honestly?

(2) If God sent a messenger in human form for you - would you listen?

honestly?

DAY 21
LUKE 2:33-35

2:33 So the child's father and mother were amazed at what was said about him. 2:34 Then Simeon blessed them and said to his mother Mary, "Listen carefully: This child is destined to be the cause of the falling and rising of many in Israel and to be a sign that will be rejected. 2:35 Indeed, as a result of him the thoughts of many hearts will be revealed—and a sword will pierce your own soul as well!"

It's apparent here that Jesus' parents were unexacting of how quickly He was coming into His calling. Secondly, we see that Mary and Jospeh are hearing that Gentiles would be saved through their son, not just Israel. This would be cause for "marveling" on their end. Lastly, a perfect stranger, Simeon, is telling them of His divine nature. We see, in the case of Simeon, *how* God has a believing people even in the worst of places, and in the darkest times. Religion was at an all time low in Israel when Christ was born. The faith of Abraham was rotting away because of the doctrines put forth by Pharisees and Sadducees. The bright light had become deplorably dim. Yet even then we find in the midst of Jerusalem a man "just and devout"--a man "upon whom is the Holy Spirit."

The phrase *the falling and rising of many* emphasizes that Jesus will bring division in the nation, as some will be judged (*falling*) and others blessed (*rising*) because of how they respond to him. The language is like Isa 8:14–15 and conceptually like Isaiah 28:13–16. Here is the first hint that Jesus' coming will be accompanied with some difficulties. Christ will be a stumbling block for many but the potential Savior of all. He is, the unilateral King of the Universe.

Read "result of Him the thoughts of many"; in this first part of the verse we are told that our thoughts will be revealed. However, this word "thoughts" is in a hostile language in the original manuscripts. The hostile thoughts we hold will be revealed. Even further, The remark *the thoughts of many hearts will be revealed* shows that how people respond to Jesus indicates where their hearts really are before God. This is a scary thought for many people, especially those who reject the Christ.

We lastly see that His words will pierce our soul like a sword. The Gospel has power and the One who commands the message is the full force behind it. The practical thought is that His premature death will brig grief toward Mary but for us, we read this and can easily apply the message to our lives. God has a way of peering into our souls and revealing what is most costly to us. The Christmas message is a joyous message but it is also a message that will bring upon a weight to our hearts. This weight must be dealt with and reasoned with. We must decide who Jesus is to us.

Challenge Question:

(1) Who is Jesus to you? Can you honestly say that He is Lord of your life?

(2) How can your Christmas time play a part in honoring Jesus?

DAY 22
ISAIAH 7:14

"Therefore the Lord Himself will give you a sign: Behold, a virgin will be with child and bear a son, and she will call His name ᵇImmanuel.

This is one of the most famous prophecies regarding the birth of Jesus the Messiah in the Bible. It also illustrates a principle of prophecy, that prophecy may have both a *near fulfillment* and a *far fulfillment*.

The *near fulfillment* of this prophecy is based around Ahaz, Jerusalem, and the attack from Israel and Syria. For Ahaz, the sign centered around a time span (**For before the Child shall know to refuse the evil and choose the good, the land that you dread will be forsaken by both her kings**). Simply stated here, God would give Ahaz a sign that within a few years, both Israel and Syria would be destroyed. This was a sign of deliverance to Ahaz.

The *far* or *ultimate fulfillment* of this prophecy goes far beyond Ahaz, to announce the miraculous virgin birth of Jesus Christ. We know this passage speaks of Jesus because the Holy Spirit says so through Matthew: "Behold, the virgin shall be with child, and bear a Son, and they shall call His name Immanuel," which is translated, "God with us." (Matthew 1:23) We know

57

this passage speaks of Jesus because the prophecy is addressed not only to Ahaz, but also to David's entire house: "O, House of David!"

Christ is the literal embodiment of the name Immanuel, "God with us", as Christ gave up eternity to enter time. He put down His royalty to become a servant. He entered humanity, which He created, only to be killed by them, in order to save them. There is no greater message than this, this is what Richard Sibbes would call "the feast of the Gospel!".

The Christmas message is the bedrock for the Gospel message. It's the miracle not just of the virgin birth which holds great theological significance but it also shows that God's love for His creation far exceeds what our minds can comprehend. John 3:16 famously depicts this and we can rest assured that God's plan was to redeem humanity to Himself once again through His faithful Son, Jesus Christ.

Challenge Questions:

(1) How do you see God with you in everyday life?

(2) Reflect in prayer the miracle that Jesus was born to save us! Have you pondered the theological significance of the Virgin Birth?

DAY 23
GALATIANS 4:4-5

4:4 But when the appropriate time had come, God sent out his Son, born of a woman, born under the law, 4:5 to redeem those who were under the law, so that we may be adopted as sons with full rights.

In the Greek language the "appropriate time" is actually read as "the fullness of time had come" which would better indicate the significance of Christ coming for Christmas. He fulfilled many prophecies, as we have seen, and many more that we have not directly mentioned in this book. Very interestingly, this is Paul's only direct reference to Jesus' virgin birth, implied in "born of a woman." Jesus was born to fulfill the law perfectly in His life and bear its curse in His death.

Born under the law Refers to Jesus' identity as a Jew. He was born into the people who lived according to God's law. Refers to the incarnation of Jesus—when the eternal Son of God became a human being (John 1:14). The fact that Jesus was born into humanity the way He was shines light on who the Jews expected to come. They thought the savior was going to be some big political giant who would free them and make them a power. However, Christ makes it clear that He is humbling himself in order to accomplish a mission from another world. He is here on behalf to His kingdom, the Kingdom of God. This is similar to when the Jews wanted a god to worship that they could see. Their expectations are human but God always has a better plan.

Verse 5 gives us an incredible amount of hope and wonder during this time of year. The Greek word used here for "redeem" is *exagorazō*, is a legal term meaning "buy out." The idea is that Christ's death has bought freedom for those who are enslaved to the law. Christ, the Lamb, came to be a purchasing sacrifice for the world. He rescued us from being subdued by the law that we could not live up to. He, who came to earth by a miracle in Mary, was the end all plan for God.

The question is raised though, this Kingdom of God, who embodies it? and who did Christ purchase? The answer lies in the Old Testament; the well-known legal procedure in the Roman Empire. The Old Testament portrays God as adopting Israel when He delivered the Hebrew people from slavery in Egypt (Exod 4:22–23; Hos 11:1) and it is in reflection here when Jesus purchases the freedom of humanity from death and sin. We are miraculously adopted from the sinful and fallen world into the glorious Kingdom of God.

That is a miracle. That brings "joy to the world". That is Christmas.

Challenge Question:
(1) Do you act more like a citizen of this world or of heaven? We should honestly apply the hope found in the Kingdom of God to our live every day - how can we better do this?

DAY 24: CHRISTMAS EVE
ROMANS 15:13

15:13 Now may the God of hope fill you with all joy and peace as you believe in him, so that you may abound in hope by the power of the Holy Spirit.

In the verse prior to this Paul references the "root of Jesse" which we learned early on this month is a prophesy of the coming Christ. Paul takes note of that here: In the original context of this quotation from Isaiah 11:10, which emphasizes that the root of Jesse will rule the nations and provide them with hope. For Paul, Jesus is the root of Jesse—the Messiah from David's line—who rules over both Jewish and non-Jewish people. All the world.

Christ starts as the root of Jesse. He is the lowest and most humble of all positions on earth. He will not remain the root forever though; He will rise. Later (in Romans), Christ is referred to as the "one who stands as the banner" - that is He will be raised for all to see. He is the root that patiently grows in humility and service but rises to take His rightful place as the banner for the world. He is the highest peak of authority and the utmost symbols of humility.

God is described as the God of Hope here and it is no mistake. The issue of evil and suffering is a long philosophical trek but at the bedrock of that mountain we know that if God is removed then hope is removed too. God brings hope through His justice, mercy and wrath but also His perfected love in Jesus Christ. From this we see the next aspect unfold that Christians should be these two spiritual things: hopeful and filled with joy that radiates peace. Not something that we do on our own but something that comes from the Holy Spirit's power alone.

This same Spirit is the Holy Spirit that protected the womb of the virgin Mary, laid His hands on Jesus during baptism and is the living God within us. The same Spirit that gives us eternal joy is the same Spirit that raised Christ from the tomb. The grace of hope, together with joy and peace in believing, are rooted in the Christian's heart, through the power of the Holy Ghost—that is, through the sanctifying influences of the Holy Spirit.

Something that is hard for me is to embody the above statements and commands. I'm often filled with anxiety and unrest over various issues coming from a fallen world. We must remind ourselves that we can abound in the power of the Spirit if we simply take these words to heart. Christmas can be hectic, wild and somewhat uncomfortable for many. There is a common thread for all of us to rejoice in though - that is Jesus, the Son of God, come to take the sins of the world.

Challenge Question:

(1) Anxiety is everywhere, do you pray that God will give you the power to cover those moments with hope?

(2) Joy is something that is mistaken for happiness. Joy is not happiness but greater - it is contentment in all situations. Pray for joy with your family and friends.

DAY 25: CHRISTMAS
ISAIAH 9:6

For a child has been born to us, a son has been given to us. He shoulders responsibility and is called: Wonderful Counselor, Mighty God, Everlasting Father, Prince of Peace.

Christ is born! Christmas is here! and we must remember that it was over a thousand years before Christ was born that He was foretold through Isaiah. We have Christmas because Christ foretold the coming of His birth through a prophet of Israel. How incredible and stunning is this?

The very next phrase is something that I've personally missed on several study occasions: "He shoulders responsibility". He alone is the one who will be responsible for the everlasting weight of sin and justice. He's been giving the authority for this responsibility from the Father and will see it through even though the weight of such burden is more than any one of us could ever imagine. It also foretells the kingship that Christ will indeed have over all of the world.

According to the Davidic Covenant (2 Sam. 7:14), the term "son" is a title for the king. The same is true in the vision of Daniel where the expression "Son of Man" is used (7:9-14). Daniel's vision shows this glorious king in the presence of the Almighty, the Ancient of Days, and that he would be given the kingdom of peace. Isaiah announces that the child to be born will be this Son given. This idea is then clarified by Paul: "In the

fullness of time, God sent forth His Son, born of a woman
... ." (Gal. 4:4).

"Wonderful" is a word that primarily describes the GOD,
YHWH, or extraordinary or supernatural things in the
Scriptures; it means "extraordinary, surpassing, marvelous,
wonderful." It was not used in a simple sense, as we often use
the English word "wonderful." To describe the king with this
Hebrew word "wonderful" would be ascribing to him
extraordinary, normally supernatural abilities. The second word
is "counselor" which means to "behold wisdom or one who
plans" and this is ever proven by the New Testament in
testimony of the Christ. John chapter 2 tells us that Christ
knows what is inside every man's heart and mind. This should
be an encouragement - Christ knows, feels and is within the
realm of help for us. He is our wonderful and mighty counselor.

This next declaration is a simple and straightforward alert
that He, Christ, holds the power of deity. In other words, He is
God, He is part of the triune God. In fact, he has just
announced in chapters 7 and 8 that this king would be known as
Immanu-'el, "God with us." To say "a king is with us" would be
of little effect. But to say that a king is coming whose power
will display that God is with the people—that is a sign.

The next name simply compounds the fact that Christ is
God. They are not separate but the same triune God. In the
first name we see that Jesus will behold the Holy Spirit, the
second one affirms His deity and the third one confirms the

trinity by compounding Christ' authority with the Father. In the last description or name of Christ, He is called Prince of Peace, which refers to Christ coming to the earth first to redeem mankind and in the second coming He will end all suffering in the New Heaven.

If this text doesn't spur hope, zeal and wonder in our hearts we must take time to truly meditate on them. This is the mist that covers Christmas morning and we must be in awe of it. This wonderful promise of a savior has come to be. Our Christ is born, Our savior has come, He has conquered this world and overcome sin for our sake. You, this Christmas, can have the confidence in Christ that we are free of sin and now becoming righteous and holy in His sight.

Amen.

CONCLUSION AND THOUGHTS

As I wrote this I kept thinking of what the main purpose was for this book. I tried to persuade myself that this was simply going to be an exegetical book for those attempting to learn the deeper end of the Christmas narrative in the Scriptures. However, as I wrote, I realized it was more than that - it was a daily attempt at focusing our hearts towards Christ during the most wonderful time of year. It's because of who Christ is that we are able to enjoy cookie making, the Christmas tree, the family time, the cider, the eggnog, the gift giving and getting. That may sound weird because all of which I mentioned is made from a tradition but the impact started with Christ and the God who came to humanity from divinity to rescue the creation that went astray.

I really do hope that this devotional finds you well. I hope that it encourages you, keeps you centered on Christ during one of the busiest times of the year. I also hope that it has a lasting effect so that you're able to enter the new year with a new found hope in Christ and His wonderful message to the world. And just maybe you'll be able to set a resolution that revolves around daily focus with Christ. I'm excited and thankful that you've read this short book and I pray that it feeds you in a wonderful way.

Merry Christmas.

Made in the USA
Lexington, KY
20 November 2018